A NOTE TO PARENTS

When your children are ready to "step into reading," giving them the right books—and lots of them—is as crucial as giving them the right food to eat. **Step into Reading Books** present exciting stories and information reinforced with lively, colorful illustrations that make learning to read fun, satisfying, and worthwhile. They are priced so that acquiring an entire library of them is affordable. And they are beginning readers with an important difference—they're written on four levels.

Step 1 Books, with their very large type and extremely simple vocabulary, have been created for the very youngest readers. **Step 2 Books** are both longer and slightly more difficult. **Step 3 Books,** written to mid-second-grade reading levels, are for the child who has acquired even greater reading skills. **Step 4 Books** offer exciting nonfiction for the increasingly proficient reader.

Children develop at different ages. **Step into Reading Books,** with their four levels of reading, are designed to help children become good—and interested—readers *faster*. The grade levels assigned to the four steps—preschool through grade 1 for Step 1, grades 1 through 3 for Step 2, grades 2 and 3 for Step 3, and grades 2 through 4 for Step 4—are intended only as guides. Some children move through all four steps very rapidly; others climb the steps over a period of several years. These books will help your child "step into reading" in style!

To Jeremy and Elaine

The snake on the facing page is a long-nosed tree snake.

Text copyright © 1994 by Lucille Recht Penner. Illustrations copyright © 1994 by Peter Barrett. All rights reserved under International and Pan-American Copyright Conventions. Published in the United States by Random House, Inc., New York, and simultaneously in Canada by Random House of Canada Limited, Toronto.

Library of Congress Cataloging-in-Publication Data
Penner, Lucille Recht.
S-S-Snakes! / by Lucille Recht Penner ; illustrated by Peter Barrett.
    p.   cm. — (Step into reading. A Step 2 book)
ISBN 0-679-84777-4 (pbk.) — ISBN 0-679-94777-9 (lib. bdg.)
1. Snakes—Juvenile literature. [1. Snakes.]
I. Title.   II. Title: Snakes!   III. Series: Step into reading. Step 2 book.
QL666.06P35   1994   597.96—dc20   93-46799

Manufactured in the United States of America   3 4 5 6 7 8 9 0

Step into Reading™

Snakes!

By Lucille Recht Penner
Illustrated by Peter Barrett

A Step 2 Book

Random House New York

A snake charmer
sits in front of a basket
and begins to play his flute.
A crowd gathers.

Slowly a big cobra
rises from the basket.
Oooh! Everyone moves back.

4

The snake charmer isn't afraid.

He sways to the music.

The cobra sways too.

Indian cobra

Is the cobra really
dancing to the music?
No.
It can't even hear it.
Snakes have no outer ears.
But the cobra watches
the snake charmer carefully.
It moves when he moves.

From the beginning of time
people have been fascinated by snakes.
This Egyptian king
lived long ago.
His headdress had
a golden cobra on it.

The cobra stood
for the king's power
to strike at his enemies.

9

A Greek story tells
of a monster called Medusa
who had snakes for hair.
Medusa was so scary
that everyone who saw her
turned to stone!

A picture of Medusa
made long ago

In another old story
soldiers were fighting
the great Roman army.
They threw clay jars filled with snakes
into Roman ships.
The jars smashed.
Snakes crawled everywhere.
The terrified Romans
gave up right away.

Even today many people
are afraid of snakes.

How strange snakes seem!
They have no arms or legs
or fur or feathers.

Their eyes never blink.

A snake slithers silently
along the ground
or wraps itself around a tree.

How can a snake do that?
Doesn't it have any bones?

Yes. A snake has 400 bones
in its back.

You have only 33 bones
in your back.

A snake's bones are connected
by joints that bend.

That's why it can turn and twist
its body into coils.

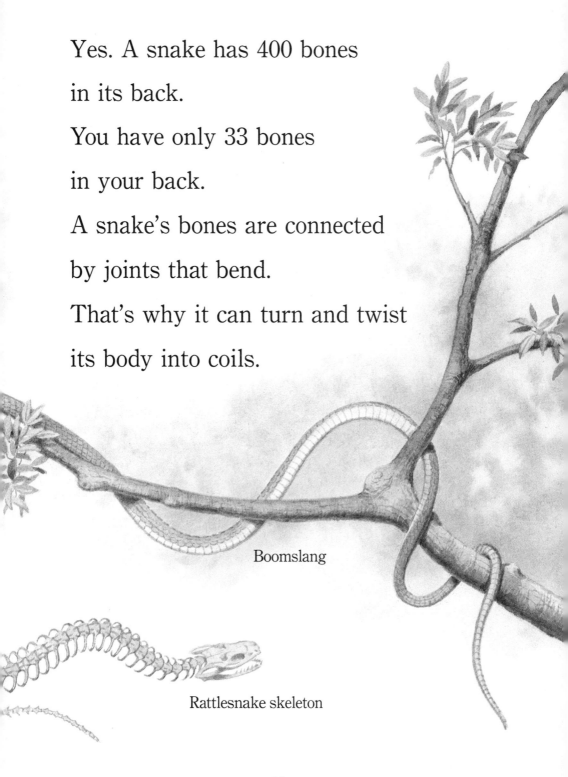

Boomslang

Rattlesnake skeleton

Banded sea snake

What can a snake do

besides crawl and climb trees?

Snakes can swim.

Paradise tree snake

Some snakes even seem to fly.

A tree snake spreads itself like a kite

and floats from branch to branch.

Snakes live almost
everywhere in the world.
But they don't live
at the North and South Poles.
It's too cold for them.

Your blood is always about
the same temperature.
A snake's blood changes
with the temperature of the air.
A snake will die
if it gets too cold
or too hot.

Western diamondback rattlesnake

Snakes that live in the hot desert
creep into holes
to hide from the sun.

When it gets cold,

it's hard to find snakes.

They sleep through the winter

in holes and caves.

It's spring!

Hundreds of snakes wake up

and slither into the sun.

Two male snakes begin to fight.

They don't bite each other.

But they raise their heads
and butt each other.

The one that gets knocked down
is the loser.

The winner mates
with a female.

European adders

Most snakes are born
in the summer.

Some snakes have live babies.

Most lay eggs.

Mother snakes don't take care
of their babies.

Little snakes have to find
their own food.

Scarlet kingsnakes

Puff adders

21

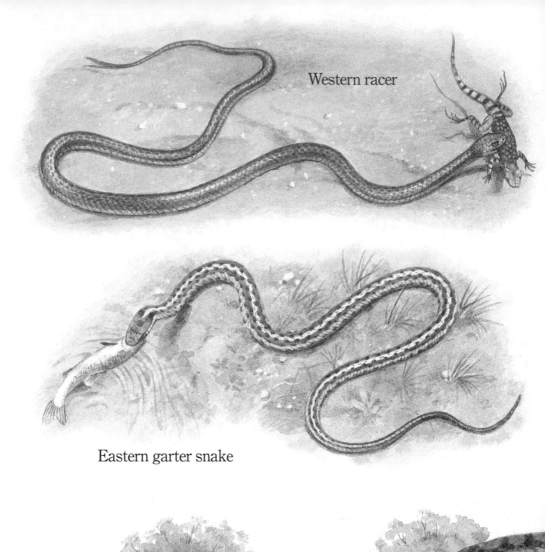

Western racer

Eastern garter snake

What do snakes eat?

Live animals!

Insects, worms, snails,

frogs, lizards, and fish.

Some snakes even eat bats.

They climb high trees near bat caves.

When the bats fly in and out,

the snakes strike.

Carpet python

The biggest snakes
can swallow a leopard
or an alligator.
It takes ten people
to hold this huge anaconda.
It is thirty feet long
and weighs more than
a hundred pounds.

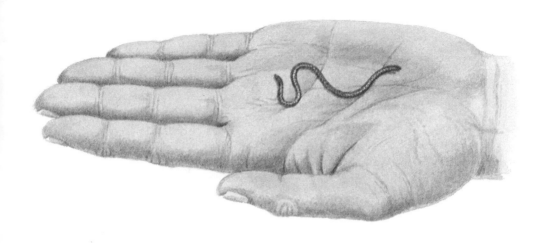

The smallest snakes
can fit in your hand.
This tiny thread snake
eats ants.

How do snakes

catch their prey?

A baby copperhead wiggles

its bright yellow tail

to attract a little mouse.

The mouse doesn't know

the tail is part of a snake.

It comes close to look.

Suddenly the mouse sees the snake.

It freezes.

It's too scared to move.

Eeek! The snake grabs the mouse

with its sharp teeth.

This African snake is stealing eggs
from a bird's nest.
The snake is only as thick
as your finger.
But it can swallow a whole egg
without cracking it!

Little spikes inside its throat
poke holes in the eggshell.
The insides run
into the snake's stomach.
Then the snake spits out
the empty shell.

African egg-eating snake

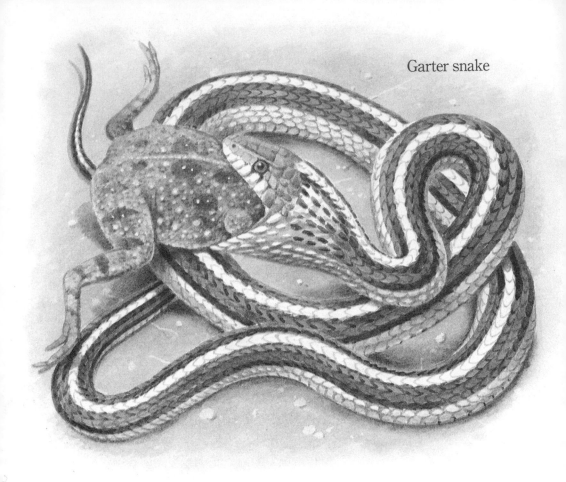

Garter snake

A snake can even stretch its jaws
wide enough to swallow an animal
larger than its head!
It swallows its prey nose first.
After a big meal, some snakes can wait
weeks or months before eating again.

Some snakes are constrictors.
They coil around their prey
and squeeze until it
stops breathing.

Ball python

Some snakes kill their prey
by poisoning it.
Snake poison is called venom.
A poisonous snake has sharp fangs.
What is a fang?
It's a hollow tooth.
When a cobra bites an animal,
venom flows through
its fangs.
After the animal dies,
the snake swallows it.

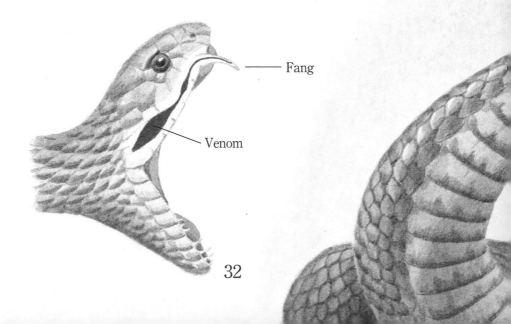

Fang

Venom

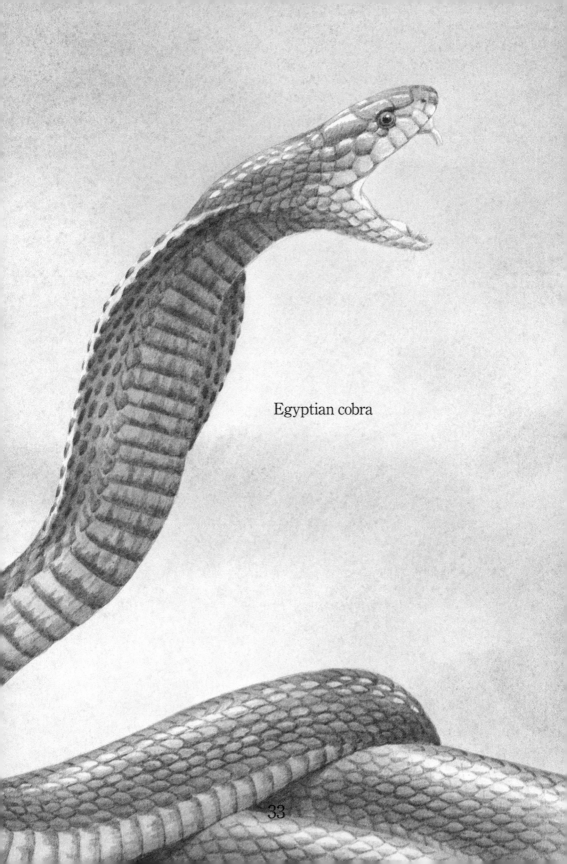

Egyptian cobra

People look and listen
when they hunt.
A snake's most important sense
is smell.
A snake flicks out
its long, forked tongue
to pick up the scent
of its prey.

Grass snake

This is a tiger snake
from Australia.
Watch out!
It's the most poisonous snake
in the world.

Pit vipers are poisonous snakes

with a special sense.

They can detect heat.

On a dark night a pit viper

can kill a mouse

without even seeing it.

Scientists tried an experiment

with a pit viper.

They filled one balloon

with cold water.

They filled another balloon

with hot water.

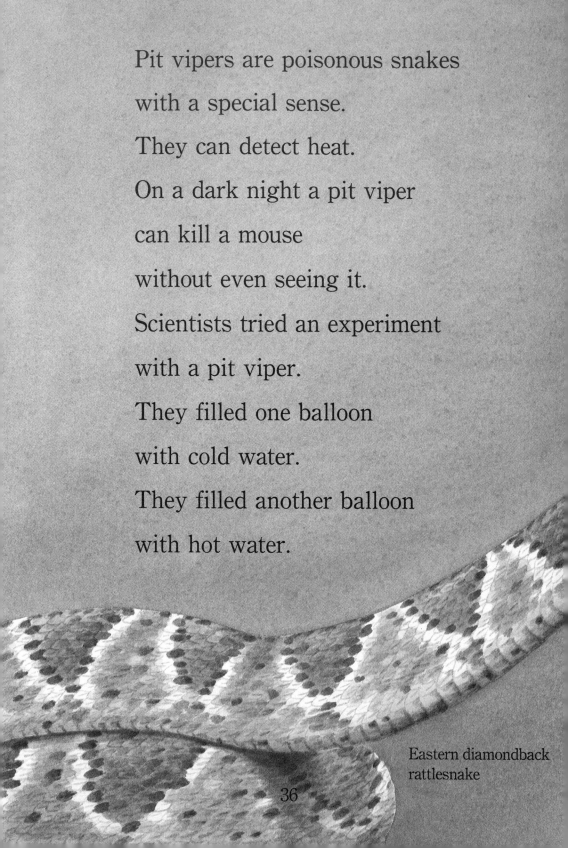

Eastern diamondback
rattlesnake

Then they turned out
the lights.
The pit viper struck
at the warm balloon
and burst it!

A rattlesnake is a pit viper.

Its tail has bands

of loose skin.

They rattle loudly when the snake

shakes its tail.

It's a scary sound.

Timber rattlesnake

The rattle is a warning:

LEAVE ME ALONE!

The snake doesn't want to fight.

It would rather scare an enemy away.

When the rattlesnake

hunts for food,

it holds its tail very still.

A lion is watching

an African spitting cobra.

Will the cobra

make a good meal?

Suddenly it spits poison

into the lion's eyes.

The lion runs away.

Its eyes burn and sting.

But the little mongoose

is often a match

for a cobra.

It rushes in and bites the snake

before it can strike.

The mongoose kills the cobra

and eats it.

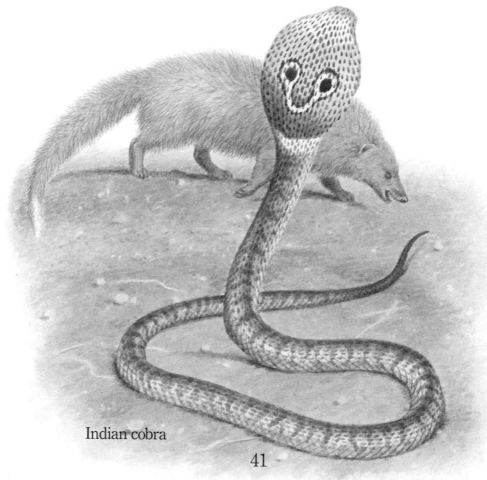

Indian cobra

Human beings are
the biggest danger to snakes.
The jungles where many snakes live
are being cut down.

Some people kill snakes
because they are afraid of them.
Large snakes are hunted
for their skins.
Snakes are disappearing
from the earth faster
than most animals.

Blanding's tree snake

Corn snake

The world needs snakes.
Snakes are part of the
balance of nature.
They eat mice and rats
that destroy our crops.

Snake venom is used
to make medicine.
The snake's head is held
over a bottle covered
with thin cloth.
The snake bites the cloth
and venom spurts
into the bottle.

Eastern diamondback
rattlesnake

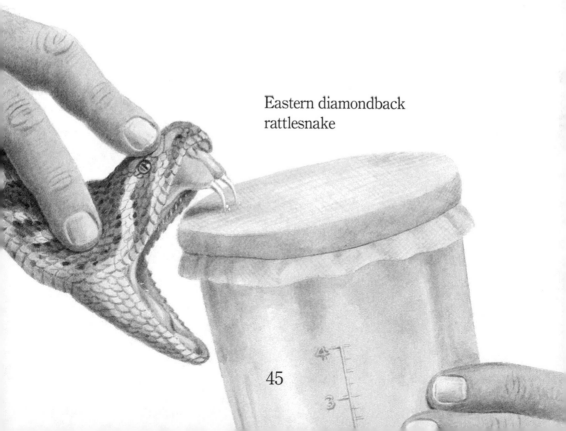

Many harmless snakes
make good pets.

Garter snakes

They are clean

and easy to care for.

Watch a snake carefully.
You may learn something
no one else knows.

Gray rat snake